Reflections

Stephen Shaw

Reflections

Stephen Shaw's Books

Visit the website: www.i-am-stephen-shaw.com

I Am contains spiritual and mystical teachings from enlightened masters that point the way to love, peace, bliss, freedom and spiritual awakening.

Heart Song takes you on a mystical adventure into creating your reality and manifesting your dreams, and reveals the secrets to attaining a fulfilled and joyful life.

They Walk Among Us is a love story spanning two realities. Explore the mystery of the angels. Discover the secrets of Love Whispering.

The Other Side explores the most fundamental question in each reality. What happens when the physical body dies? Where do you go? Expand your awareness. Journey deep into the Mystery.

Reflections offers mystical words for guidance, meditation and contemplation. Open the book anywhere and unwrap your daily inspiration.

5D is the Fifth Dimension. Discover ethereal doorways hidden in the fabric of space-time. Seek the advanced mystical teachings.

Star Child offers an exciting glimpse into the future on earth. The return of the gods and the advanced mystical teachings. And the ultimate battle of light versus darkness.

The Tribe expounds the joyful creation of new Earth. What happened after the legendary battle of Machu Picchu? What is Christ consciousness? What is Ecstatic Tantra?

The Fractal Key reveals the secrets of the shamans. This handbook for psychonauts discloses the techniques and practices used in psychedelic healing and transcendent journeys.

Reflections offers mystical words for guidance, meditation and contemplation. Open the book anywhere and unwrap your daily inspiration.

Important: Unlike my first four books, this is not a novel; instead you simply dip into the book and find your reflection for the day. Each reflection is a shimmering light along the mystical pathway toward peace, joy and bliss. For the expanded and in-depth spiritual teachings, read my books I Am, Heart Song, Star Child and They Walk Among Us.

Cover art: 'Jay' by Stephen Shaw. Copyright © 2013 Stephen Shaw.

Jay is the extraordinary mystical being mentioned in my first book I Am. Here are excerpts that described him:

"Pure white hair cascading over his shoulders, white eyebrows, white moustache, white eyelashes and amazing almond-shaped piercing blue eyes … he sure looks different to anyone I have ever seen."

"He shakes my hand and peaceful sensations stream into my body, leaving me a little light-headed."

"I feel Jay's hand on my shoulder and there is a rush of energy. Everything around me becomes still."

"There are many of us who travel from the Light to assist different realities, including your world. I am one of those beings."

Life is like holding
a beautiful rose,
gorgeous to look at
and lovely to smell,
but the thorns will
make your fingers
bleed if you hold on
too tightly.

The secret is learning
to let go and stay in
the moment.

If you don't let go of
your past, you will not
be fully present
in the Now.

Are you truly happy?
Are you full of joy?

The lie that You Are Not Good Enough naturally leads to the deception that You Must Change or You Must Be Fixed. These messages are the disease of your society.

Do you think this tree
here looks at that tree
there and decides
I Am Not Good
Enough? That I
should be bigger or
smaller or greener like
the other tree?

A white lotus simply exists. It does not look at another flower and compare, desire, label or judge. The lotus does not struggle to grow or change. It just is. Every day of its life, it simply is.

You cannot be
anything other than
who you are.

Trees don't stand around comparing heights. Flowers don't compare colours.

There is a great power
in total acceptance.

Should and Is cannot
live together.

Meditation is a path that can lead to bliss and peace, affecting your relationships, your work, your society and your world in profound and magnificent ways.

Meditation is
something you do
anytime, anywhere. It
is a pure, free practice
that is not aligned
with any ideology
or belief system.

Everything you
believe, all your
values, every bit of
your socialisation and
conditioning, every
feeling and emotion –
all these are just
thoughts flying across
the sky of your mind.

Every one of your
thoughts and feelings
are birds circling the
sky of your mind.
Instead of denying,
escaping or trying
to move these birds,
your only job is to
watch them.

Meditation is simply watching the birds.

Meditation is about
being, not doing.
You cannot chase it.
How can you
watch harder?

The more you notice,
the more you witness,
the more you
become Aware,
and the more fully
alive you become.
You are, in fact,
entering into
Existence itself.

You are already Here.

Most people are brilliant at being busy. And even when they sit still for a moment they are mentally somewhere else, usually ruminating about the past, planning some future or just daydreaming.

There is nothing but
this moment. There
is only Now.

Every time you
wallow in the past,
caught up in should
haves, could haves
and why didn't I's,
you lose your
precious connection
with Now.

Every time you
sacrifice this moment
to spend time in your
surmised future or
fantasies you lose
your connection
with Life.

There is only this precious moment. When you learn to fully step into the Now, you will discover a peace that surpasses understanding.

All of Life is contained in this moment, in the space between your thoughts, in the pause between your breaths.

There is a time for
doing and a time
for planning, but
let not your mind
be your master.

The whole of Life,
and the whole
of Existence,
is contained
in the Now.

You are an
expression of Life.

You are Life itself
pulsating in this
dimension.

When you discover
your true nature, you
will know that you
are free.

Have you ever
watched a film, and
for a few moments
become so immersed
in the story that you
forgot who you are
and where you are?

Consciousness takes
on the disguise of
forms until it loses
itself in them.
And at some point
Consciousness
awakens.

What is upsetting
you? Their actions or
your thoughts about
their actions?

Who is creating your reality?

All your thoughts
colour your vision
and alter your
perception of
Reality As It Is.

It is what it is.

All conflict is the
result of stories
clashing.

If you are truly aware, truly present, truly conscious, then you can simply notice your stories and notice other people's stories. They are just stories. Just birds in the sky.

Model the behaviour you wish to see and experience.

Witness not just
your thoughts and
emotions (your inner
world) but also the
information coming in
through your senses
(your outer world).
Otherwise you will
be trapped in your
chattering mind.

No-Mind or the Space
Between Thoughts
often occurs in the
moment when you
are fully present,
in the moment
when you are fully
conversing with
Reality As It Is.

There is only Now.
The past and future
are merely a dream.

You can use your
Now to learn from
the past and to plan
your future but as
soon as the learning
and planning are
complete, return
to the Now.

All of Life is
contained in
the Now.

What is really
important?
What will you take
with you in the end?
What, at this moment,
is lacking?

There is only
Here and Now,
and everything is a
Thought of Life.

Radical acceptance
means accepting
Reality As It Is
and then taking
responsible Action.

Accept then Act.

Meditation is simply compassionate awareness of your thoughts and feelings, and compassionate awareness of other's thoughts and feelings.

Make compassion
your first choice.
When judgement and
anger arise, take a
deep breath and view
with compassionate
understanding.

Keep practising what
you have learned. The
teachings are simple.
The rest is up to you.

You are nothing but a wave rolling on the ocean of Life. As waves, we rise up from the endless ocean, create some white foam and noisy splashes, and dissolve back into the ocean.

We are all part of the same ocean, even though each wave appears different and sounds unique.

Why not let each
wave just be, and if
you are fully present
with a particular
wave it will fulfill
its purpose and
then subside.

The greatest gift you
can give to others is
being completely
present in the
moment and
truly listening to
who they are and
what they say.

There are only
two paths to
enlightenment:
Love and Awareness.

To truly Love,
you have to die
to your self.

To be fully Aware,
you will lose
everything and find
emptiness.

Everything is
consciousness and
everything is energy.

I Am

The universe is one
unbounded ocean of
consciousness – You.

Love is Life
meeting Itself.

Love is the
Awakening.

Love is coming Home.

If you have found the
Light within yourself,
there is nothing
more in this whole
Existence to find.

Do you love
what you do?

There is living and
there is making
a living.

You are here to thrive,
not merely survive.

Discovering you means stripping away the confusing demands, expectations and labels of your parents, society, culture, religion and the media … and looking deep within to find your innate traits, talents and dispositions.

Stephen Shaw

The more you
discover you, the
more you will hear
your Heart Song.

Your Heart Song is
the essence of you.

Your Heart Song is
the beautiful melody
playing deep inside
your soul.

Your Heart Song is
your true guiding
light in this life.

Every moment of
every day you choose
the life you are living.

Your future is the
result of the choices
you make now.

Every great journey
starts with a great
root of faith and a
great cloud of doubt.

You need to accept
what is in your life.
Then begin to change
what you can, creating
steady ripples in your
Sphere Of Influence.

Sometimes you will only be able to move in tiny, incremental steps to reach a dream. Sometimes you can only change one small thing, then another, then another.

One of the biggest
secrets of reaching
a dream is
steadfastness,
determination and
patience.

What is your dream?
What is the reality
you wish to create?
How much do you
want it? Are you
willing to face the
challenges? Are you
prepared to pay
the price?

Do you have a clear
intention? Have you
painted the dream?

If your vision is clear
and your commitment
is strong, you will
enter into flow
and start to attract
synchronicities into
your life.

Do what is
necessary ... then do
what is possible ...
and slowly you
discover that you
are manifesting
your dream.

When you are in
the flow, you feel
peaceful; you sense
that you are on
the right path.

You only reach a
dream or fulfil a
vision through
determined and
gradual action
over time.

There is no failure,
only learning.
What can you do
differently next time?

Be open to feedback.
Adjust your course.

Life is about
prioritising. Choose
carefully. Follow
your heart.

Notice when something or someone connects deeply with your soul. The wise person seizes those opportunities.

You need to be clear
about what you want
in life, and what
you are prepared
to live without.

Learn to live with
deep gratitude.

What are you giving
to the world? What
will you leave behind
when you are gone?

The secret is to do it, not speculate about it.
If you want to experience deep and lasting fulfilment, you have to take action.

There are many
dimensions. You
are focusing your
consciousness in just
one or two.

You are an expression
of Life. You exist
across many
dimensions. In fact,
you exist across
all dimensions.

Each level of
expanded awareness
brings a heightened
understanding but
also another veil.
It can take a lifetime,
indeed many
lifetimes, to penetrate
the veils of the
Mystery.

Surrender and flow,
surrender and flow.

The gods of light, the precursors of the great religions, the great spiritual teachers – they all taught the same things: loving-kindness, compassion, forgiveness, acceptance, equality, respect, responsibility, gratitude and service.

What kind of reality do you wish to create?

Your first allegiance
is to Light, Love
and Truth.

You are responsible
for your own journey
toward the Light.
The goal, if you
choose it, is your own
ascension and your
own awakening.

Fully accept yourself,
radiate your inner
light and trust that the
right partner will
gravitate toward you.

The journey of Tantra
is the wildest
exposure of one's own
heart and the most
loving acceptance of
another's heart.

Courage. Forgiveness.
Vulnerability. Putting
aside hurt and pain
and risking it
all again.

Your job is to bloom –
for yourself and
for the world.

Words are empty.
Actions count.

Shine your light and
trust that it will bring
transformation.

There are two aspects to Life. The one is the underlying Source, the almost ubiquitous unmanifested Field of Dreams. The other is the infinite realities, the manifested dreams.

Life is essentially
one big orgasm
of the Heart.

You are both the
dream and the
Dreamer.

Fear will not
serve you.

Love is always
worth it.

God is the Source, the
underlying Is-ness,
the Creator of
everything. A deep
ocean that gives rise
to infinite waves.
Your reality is merely
one of these waves.

All life is a journey, a
progression and a
gradual return to
the Source.

You are consciousness
and your intention
directs your journey.

Our souls are primed for connection, compassion and companionship, and we will never be truly happy unless we live with altruism.

Altruism is the
selfless concern for
the well-being
of others.

Simplicity and spontaneity.

Speed Limit Warp 7

Walk with purpose
and leave no
footprints on other
people's souls nor on
the sacred earth.

Your mind and beliefs
act as a filter, limiting
your perception of
All That Is.

We are energy beings
interacting in an
energy world.

The secret is to keep
your energy clear.

Live the
impeccable life.

Walk in peace
with the world.

Accept what is,
change what you can.

Love unconditionally.

Let go of judgements.

Operate with
radical respect
to all living beings.

You are responsible
for your life and
your choices.

There are many
realities on the
way to the Source.
You choose your
own journey.
It all depends on
what you seek,
what you desire.

There are abundant
resources on this
planet, more than
enough for everyone.
They just need to
be shared.

How can you alleviate the suffering of fellow humans?

Find joy in the little
things: The whisper
of a gentle breeze,
the sun on your skin,
the smell of the ocean,
the grass underfoot,
a flower in your hair,
a song in your heart,
a butterfly in your
hand.

Life is beautiful.
Love conquers all.
(It may, however,
require a little
patience)

The moment you truly accept and love another being, that being becomes a mysterious reflection of Yourself.

Life is a series of
stories that you create
in order to learn
about Love.

Love Whispering is
the secret ingredient
of joyful relationships.

It's all about surrendering into Love. And acting with Love.

In the end there is only Love and Light.